Threads

BOOKS BY JEFFREY ROUND

POETRY

In the Museum of Leonardo da Vinci

FICTION

A Cage of Bones
The Honey Locust
Endgame

THE BRADFORD FAIRFAX MYSTERIES

The P-Town Murders, Death in Key West,
Vanished in Vallarta, Bon Ton Roulet

THE DAN SHARP MYSTERIES

Lake on the Mountain, Pumpkin Eater,
The Jade Butterfly, Shadow Puppet,
After the Horses, Lion's Head Revisited,
The God Game

Threads:

A Poetry Collection

by

Jeffrey Round

Beautiful Dreamer Press

Beautiful Dreamer Press
309 Cross Street
Nevada City, CA 95959
U.S.A.
www.BeautifulDreamerPress.com
info@BeautifulDreamerPress.com

"Turn" first appeared in *The Antigonish Review*; "Friends" and "Father" first appeared in *The New Quarterly*; "Autumn Lessons" first appeared in *The Prairie Journal of Canadian Literature*; "Small Furies" first appeared in *Canadian Literature*; and "Rebel" first appeared in *I Found It at the Movies*.

Paperback Edition
10 9 8 7 6 5 4 3 2 1
Printed in the United States of America
Publication date: March, 2022

ISBN: 978-1-7347389-9-5
Library of Congress Control Number: 2021948146

Cover design by Inkspiral

For my friends and lovers
past / present / future
who run through these poems
like a river running
through a landscape
brimming with possibilities

CONTENTS

Part I

Small Furies

Part II

Nights of Pleasure

Part III

Three Confessional Poems

Part IV

The James Dean Poems

Part V

Threads

Threads:
A Poetry
Collection

PART I

Small Furies

EINE KLEINE NACHTMUSIK
(A LITTLE NIGHT MUSIC)

Would you hear it again?
effervescent in the dusk like the whine
    of silken candles
each his own

draw back the blade
peel off the skin and douse the flame

a silver drop

LOT'S WIFE

Love is that thing we dare
           not touch
dare not extract from
                   the past
exploding now behind us

Our footsteps echo with
               cries
of the ones left behind
let me go to them

Love is a body
it has a fragrance all its own
it is clear and hard
           though
I cannot touch it
cannot hide when
you look at me, husband

We had no warning,
no time to learn death
before they came to our gates
with their edicts from a god
           so mighty
ordering us
to leave our homes
in the name of salvation

What god can want such a thing
this destruction
of relatives, my brothers, young Daniel
how can I leave them
what nature is this so hard
that calls for our blood?

The old women tell us
to dream is more dangerous
than to touch these angry days
as my hand reaches out
to take hold firmly
my scarf fluttering in the wind,
I must hold it down
like a flag become
too noticeable

This earth, this clay so shapely
impels me forward
as I move in my mind's eye
backward to the city
hastening to worn walls
to find warmth, learn the
            escaped

My pots and vessels of oil,
the garlic wreaths hung to dry
will not be there when we return

Long after the wind
            traces our path
through these canyons
to the hills beyond
will love follow
as I falter now at your heels,
husband-father?

Husband—catch me!
my hands are warm and elusive
to each her own way down

I turn and tremble
move into stone

SMALL FURIES

Beware silence
distrust stillness
things that lie beneath the surface
do not seem

Death leaps up sudden
like trout from still water
snatching flies mid-air
or a car over-leaping the banks
of a sidewalk
pedestrians scattered
mid-stream

FATHOM FIVE

The face of   death
moves
        sudden
like   thought or
possible
              images
in the window
pane
            (shattered)
       reflections
in the wink
  of time
brief days
      snapping
       shut

Now enfeebled we see
backwards
      through what
we once   knew
memories
   hovering   black
     angels
in naked
          light
reality has
no depth
down here
where the dead men play

Betrayal
blends with the seasons
as we sit
on park benches

[9]

old cast-offs
though love still harpoons us
spears us in the gullet
knows the fault lines of
drooling mouths
    and weary hearts

Strange how we
learn
    to move limbs
like false   hopes
buoys
        that guide
      hands of horror
        still
reaching out
we never forget
    all
we used to be
when we were
      young

PREPARATIONS FOR ARRIVAL

I rehearse my dying
establish its rhythms
its small victories
daily

I know how to approach
death in many ways
without ever arriving

Dying is an event
like any other
a date to mark on
the calendar
like the foreclosure of
something smaller
than a house

There is someone
living within
who am I now?

The symptoms are frightful
I am not who I am
I cannot be myself in this
company I keep

If I look in the mirror
death is the idea
facing me there
I have gone beyond need

Salvation keeps
such strange company

Bowls of fruit, warm milk
I eat for two
but consume less to conserve
space inside me
I am a simultaneity
my shadow lives within

Death is a considerate lodger
he knows my ins and outs
installs himself bit by bit
insinuating himself in my heart
like a beautiful lover

It's like living under glass
the bell will chime presently
to let us know the ether
is in place, the jar closed

Sanctuary

He is a good guest, after all
has warm hands, clean habits
though they do not
coincide with mine
perhaps we will
learn each other's ways
living together so intimately

What could be finer?
we are keen to know
one another,
like old friends
getting re-acquainted
after many years apart

We use each other

It is not frightful
merely unforgiving
and relentless

To be known so intimately
is a strange seduction

How is it once again
love
has got the better of me?

STRANGE LAND

Sir, I am a tourist here
an explorer in this place
whose paths go nowhere
whose crossroads lead only to
other crossroads

I am mute as a mountain
silent as a night sky
crooked as a field of crosses
plain as dirt
and simple as water

I labour to excavate
the Mausoleum of Love
heeding the whispers of
childhood that said
one day all would be well
though clearly
uttered only to placate

Lead us on then
to this land without shores
this place where
we step off the map
into dark water, endless night

JOURNEY

Leave your suitcase by the door
you won't need it here
you have no right to life
or any reminders of that now
you are just another inmate
close your eyes and make of this room
what you will

Put your fear in that drawer
sorrow's too rare a commodity to last,
like a lily in a vase
under all this lingering

You may keep your soft melancholy
and your silent regrets, fog-like and still
even Lazarus has had his try of it
and will not be back

At first, in the desert
a hard time we had
and cold at night
red   cloud   dust
scratching new surfaces, strange pills
but the water we found was bitter
and hard to drink
from freezing and thawing and freezing again
warming our hands round cups of tea
we sink into   dusk early
like birds fleeing darkness

Your words are leaves
vanishing on the wind

though you press them to my face
and hold them to my eyelids
like petals

Light a fire
make a thought form in your mind
then place it between us
you are already far away
as I fasten my harsh mouth upon it
seizing on a handful of dry syllables
someday someone may attempt to interpret
these hieroglyphs of love

After the long night
dawn makes me giddy with its terrifying buzz
like a committee decided at last
or an infinite number of wishes
about to come true
we have been lured here by a bright candle
snuffed out and left for dead

The ninth day:
        warmer, gentle and fair
we are nearly there, I say
but there is no heart in my words
only air and empty graces
saved for an end
that never comes

Things shimmer on the edge of the room
like a mirage on a sand dune
giving pale comfort
while ant-like we crawl through
    wind and rain

for you:
      almonds, hibiscus flowers bloom
in a white season
as you clutch at your hands

Kiss this empty skull
then use it for a rattle
on the end of a stick
shards   stains   bruises
everywhere the remnants
    of a hard tourist trade
if I carve my initials in bone
a femur, perhaps someone
will use it as a walking stick

Outside my window
a bell tolls the hour:
    one if by water
    two if by air
I have heard they will come
by candlelight to take us

COLD SWEATS 4 A.M.

Piss pot glows gold
in mute surrender
to the syllabus of doom
pouring from my loins
full fathom five

In the mirror
sweat glistens
like stars over distant hills
too fearful or far-off
to be taken for rain
night prowls like
tiger-ache in my bones
whose fearful touch
says love is not
to be trusted

Nether shards of grief
dull with nightdamp
    urine smell
of vinegar
mince like a waltzing deb

Eyes gleam embers
in the face of hell
    fire of living
a wick snuffed
in a black room
    stench now

Strength
    is a light switch
out of reach
to this feeble child's hand
new to gripping

In the brief lull
of night's heat
is simple knowing
between myself
    and
nothingness   exists

A single spark

PART II

Nights of Pleasure

DAVID

Nights I've lost in the
splendour of you, my lips
pressed against your skin
to suck out the stains
of my desire.

How I loved your belly,
fell into its cool sway like a
field of snow, as children
lean into whiteness
to describe passing angels.

From vanity I fashioned you,
caught God's handiwork in marble,
while cold stone floated
to life beneath my hands.

Still, you defeated me,
shut me away from your warmth,
and the blood flowing
behind your eyes.

Undeterred, I closed my mind to
the universe's dull drivel,
chipping and scraping away at flesh,
knowing one small taste of you
could stop my babble, as silt
stops up my mouth.

Just so, I unstoned my desire,
let semen flow across sere lips
rolling down like paint
from the Sistine ceiling.

When His Holiness sees me next,
he will be foul
over this giant I have conquered,
this flesh made word.
What punishment will be my reward
for having created a god
in man's image?

He won't understand
what lies between us.
He'll plot to unschool your beauty,
hating me for what
he cannot have, envying
how I touch you,
bring you to life till you cry:

Behold, I am a man!
Flesh me with your desire.
Creator, love me!

And so will he be struck dumb
to hear all of God's longing
unleashed in a single cry.

NIGHTS OF PLEASURE
(FOR JON)

Nights of pleasure come
far fewer now
that I am older, amigo

But your cock inside me is *duro*,
a raging stallion
that makes me feel secure
and strong

And when you cum
my body fills with stars

A VIRGO CONTEMPLATES PERFECTION

Seen from below, those massive thighs
could be the Pillars of Hercules—
the smooth abdominals leading up
to the *ne plus ultra* of the pectorals,
which look from afar to be hairless, yet
are anything but. Covered in fine blonde
mesh, they are at odds with the statue's
coarse skin, the wiry stubble of cheeks and chin.

Those eyes—are they green, hazel or violet?
It's so hard to decide. For the love of
Dionysus, this has to be more than a quickie!
There is too much here to take in at once,
too much to contemplate in a single glance.

What manner of god parented this voluptuous
gargantuan, this *pater familias*, parting my rosy
lips and slipping his tongue down my throat
to let loose a rain of saliva?

God almighty, what manner of man is this
whose phallus slams like a jackhammer,
stitching me together and ripping me apart
at the same time? Ye gods, how he loves
to plunge and dip, taking me to places
I've only dreamed of—all the way to Knossos
and back with each ecstatic thrust.

Heavens, what he can do with that stamen,
those orbs hanging down, each one golden
and perfect. This is what I've been seeking,
night after night, for how many years now?

It's too much, too much! It can't get any
better as he tilts me up and embraces me,
releasing a jet stream of molten fuel
then sighs and lays back. I don't resist.
For he is sublime. Master to slave,
never was there better.

It's just gone three. The bell tolls. So now
the towel—here it comes—and the trousers
hiked back into place. And there he goes,
leaving me alone to contemplate a life
to be lived after such perfection.

Of the twelve labours of Hercules, surely
these are the greatest! Now I can say
I have stolen the apples of the Hesperides
and captured the Cretan bull.

VON GLOEDEN

You, ethnographer of Sicily
Witness to these shining moments
Glowing bits of time:
This boy's back, another's foot
Resting on his thigh, one hand
Thrown casually over a shoulder
Moments suffused with the sacred,
Thermopylae in robes
Palms swaying to a moment's caress

Gauging the balance between
Poetry and the reality of these
Peasants, fishermen and shepherds
Tauroménion, home to artists and lovers
Ardently thirsting for beauty
As your lens brings the centuries
Into sharp focus

Resurrecting legends with your
Dreamy boys, here is one so versed in song
It's as if Pan had come to life

In this, we scarcely notice
The leopard-skin throw
Beneath the boy with beautiful thighs
The classical poses as though the gods
Were in mourning for their former lives
Casting a glance over the balustrade to the sea
Where a lover is only now
Returning from war unscathed

Or here, dirty Dionysus grinning in rags
As these two boys, like blushing brides
Hold flowers between them
A fig leaf on the younger's head

Now here's your favourite, Il Moro
With his penis like a fist
Unfurled for your yearning eye
All this boyish beauty given
For a smile and a camera's soft click

TOUGH

this boy, this young
tough
is highly sexual
but what he is not
and can never be
is beautiful
the broken nose, frizzy
hair, bad teeth
he knows he is hard
sitting there
on his bike, arms held
loosely at his sides
yet his small pink nipples
are rosebuds soft as a spring
morning
they do not disdain
my carnal gaze
do not censor my
awkward lust on finding
this libidinous jewel on a
street corner
rather
they invite me to
look, touch, smell
they ask me
to let him in

POEM FOR A CARDIOLOGIST

You were such a mystery to me,
with your strong, clean profession and your
bright stethoscope and your ability to glean
the rhythms of life.

I was astonished to learn you could
interpret the hearts of the men you were with.
Is yours the profession of love then?
Can you read a pulse like a voice on the
phone, listen for the soft trills of joy
that tell me you are here inside me?

I smiled you a star each morning
we were apart, counting the days
till my return, brave warrior, while
my hands longed to grasp your chest,
firm nipples chiselled like clefts in
rock for me to climb you.

No words on the phone could console
me for my pain, for missing your touch,
you far away in snow and me in a
restaurant on Isla Mujeres between
two friends, one an ex-lover,
who had never heard your name.

In the background, the ocean spread
its gentle waves, telling me to wait
patiently, while your voice in my head
played over and over in the soft
rhythms of evening like a pulse
spreading through everything.

Doctor, here is my heart. Heal me.

INTIMATIONS OF MORTALITY
(FOR TRENT HURRY)

Surprised to find within my breast
A heartbeat flutter from of old,
I lay my hand upon his head
And cried the tears that did unfold.

But you were ever gay, I said,
Though nay are not now so.
And my sweet soul has gone and fled
To find thee here and now.

I smiling kissed his hoary lips
And smoothed his wrinkled brow
Then fast turned up those sullen lids
And loved the smile that death undid.

O QUESTION NOT THE ONE I LOVE

O question not the one I love
Though he be nothing wondrous fair
His hair not gold, his lips not red
His prick an outing to despair.
My carnal thoughts for him are plain
They boast of nothing more than sex
And while with him I ride the stag
My love and life he both doth vex.

THE MILKY WAY UNINTENDED

They had not been gone long
   but outside the car was light
shining over Ostler's Green
from all those places
   crowded with stars
scarves and scarves of it
billowing
     radiant and green
falling through the air
as though meant
   just for them
in the soft afterglow
     of the universe reset with a switch
serenely furious
       like a far-off dream
    or an S-O-S
from some long-forgotten god

PART III

Three Confessional Poems

FRIENDS

You once said, Trust
me at your peril—
I use all my friends.
I laughed, called you
friend and trusted you
just the same.

When your second
boyfriend in six months
threw you out,
I took you in
with the warning:
I'm impossible
to live with.
To prove me right,
you convinced my boyfriend
of the same.
Within a month
he was gone.

That same month, I
introduced you to
my world: boss,
co-workers, friends,
brought you happily
on board at work.
You were diligent and good.
My boss declared you
the most interesting person
he'd met that year.
Doubtless, he'd counted.
He was that kind of dull.

Within a year
I was gone.
You whispered sweet nothings
in his ear, convincing him
you would be better
in my place.
And so you were.

Later, we mourned the loss
of lovers, other friends
one at a time.
I saw you often at the chapel,
knelt near you in cemeteries
those cool September days,
the rituals adding up.
I could write a book of
remembrance, a bible
brought to a slow boil.

Now, when I see you,
eyes averted, we pass
like two unknowns
fearing to connect.
Flesh hard, our past
weak from the burning
between us.

I see your dying eyes,
thinning veins, haunted face.
I know your number:
a street with no name.
I would call you back,
sit in orchards
of our youth under
cherry blossoms with you,

remembering us together.
Use me now, friend.

FATHER

I watch my father sleep—
dull, sunken eyes
a hand flapping restlessly
like a dying moth
under sheets the colour of remorse

This old man, drawn up firm
like a shrunken walnut
curled in its shell
is all that remains
of my great teacher, my enemy
ghost of my short-lived past

I never asked his forgiveness
for my lack of understanding
how he raised four sisters
and a mother, a rake-thin teenager
with the only stable income in a
father-less family

I never asked about the Christmas
without a tree, without food
but for a basket of oranges
donated by a kindly neighbour

I never showed sorrow
for making him beat me
for stealing
just for the fun of it
foolishly getting caught
when he would never
have stolen
even to survive

I showed no repentance
for being ashamed of him
by his dress, his speech
as though it were
an insult to my dignity,
like a lesson in what
I hoped not to be

Old man, we never talked
had nothing to discuss
father-to-son
though my dislike for you
was loud and clear
I respected nothing of your world
took everything for my own

Father, as you lie
dreaming your dreams of
dull remembrance—
can you hear me now?

Autumn Lessons

Reading these poets again
resurrected from my youth,
I recognize in the light
of late afternoon
what I missed then,
took for holy what was
justly ordinary:
Auden's *Good-bye to the Mezzogiorno*,
for instance, charts
a simple walk with his lover
in a country whose geography
I have since travelled often;
that his lover was a man
is something I barely reflect on now.
Ondaatje's *Secular Love*,
a song of plaintive longing
to his mysterious mistress,
is about a woman I now know
well enough to call at home,
beautiful, but human no less.

I am getting to know my way
around at last.
My dog who jumps for joy
at the door each night
when I return
may be offering his love,
but is probably hoping
for a friendly hand,
a quick walk around the block
all the same.

Those beautiful boys
with ample thighs and big,
rounded buttocks
so secure, so masculine
once so foreign to me,
I now see for what they are:
the pleasurable vessels of
summery evenings.
Their smiles are
the smiles of insecure boys
who, like me,
underestimated themselves
in their simple desires,
now longed for, now forgotten
by other boys
just like them.

PART IV

The James Dean Poems

REBEL

(On Re-viewing Nicholas Ray's *Rebel
without a Cause*)

remark
how
  or when
you are moved
  touched
by a
    red
    jacket
hair   comb   stained t-shirt
    slicked back
      the stars
    tapping out a beat
watching   count   down
      to
            fade

not knowing   when sound ends
    how lights flicker up
like morning
    we rise   slowly
      for the sun
        not to shine
        stumble to stand
      down the stairs
past the bleached-out popcorn stand
    like ruins
filtering through corridors
    of lost time

light filters through   the arched sphere
            does not us touch
        it moves away
            among the cars
            reckless teenagers
        things we cannot touch
            cannot become
            behind us

        the mustachioed gentleman in blue
            face a pale moon
        stands
            fending off the movie's end
        as something akin to a nervous condition
            schizophrenia
            past   present
        ushers us through   portals
            to a nervous future
        hesitant beat   stamped
            on empty sky

        how picked-to-the-bone we feel
            afterward
        as we start off   one thing
            slowly   filtered down
        to become another
                    standing
        careless   caressless
                where
        what has become isolated
        are these things that inform us
            of our being
        the things that matter

and find we have become
   those lost objects:
      pocket comb
   stolen
            gun
      red   jacket
   place in time
         increasingly

   staggering out of existence

JAMES DEAN INCOMPLETE

You sit and watch his/your
adolescence up on the screen,
not in triple X but in
a time before your dreams were formed

long before they became calcified with
regret.

You, James Dean—
you are James Dean.

Too old for his/your young skin,
it is his finest hour.
It is yours.

Only he is living and you are dead—
No, that's not right!

He is only alive on screen
yet you, somehow, are less alive
than he

as he kisses Julie Harris
high up on the Ferris wheel
breaking her heart and yours.

Somehow
his death becomes your death
leaving you
to wonder where his/your life has
gone and why

you couldn't have gone with
him when he went.

An Elegy for James Dean

Your image fills the screen
big, larger than life
and luminous, distorted
by my mind's eye, all
the discontent of you,
ragged, commanding
something more than
a mere boy, street urchin
with a fiery star at your heart

Sometimes in the evening
I pull the dagger from my side,
shore up the wound
and disguise the blood
to go looking for you
who bear my cross
though I never find you
or never recognize you
if I do

I am a sad scout
a hustler of lost dreams
exhuming you
as you flicker and fade
before my eyes
trailing after you
to Eden or Marfa

Like a child in a fairy tale
I follow the trail of crumbs,
clues to your existence

In my study at home
I keep a piece of bark
from a long-dead tree
whose boughs you once
climbed as a boy
a small rock from
your death star, the
site where you crashed
forever exploding
into light

DEATH OF A LEGEND

There he is, the legend
now grown rank and feeble
pointed out by girls in
the Warner Brothers
cafeteria line:
> *Mr. Dean, will you sign*
> *my autograph book?*
> *Mr. Dean, will you*
> *give me a kiss? Sigh!*

His once-luminous career crippled
by a series of flops:
> a boxing picture
> a screwball comedy
> a western (that
> disastrous collusion
> with John Wayne.)

Well now there then
he says, coy as ever.
Once the new Brando,
he's grown fat and bloated.
Who'd ever have thought
the "rebel" would
cash in his chips?

Don't you know
rebels are supposed
to die young?
You've disgraced
yourself—it's back
to wardrobe with you.

Shuffling and mumbling,
stumbling over the
horizon with the
other dinosaurs:
        Crawford and Davis,
        Gable and Monroe
        just waiting to make a
        mockery of their careers
        for one last grasp
        at the limelight.

Fallen, unable to rise
he lifts his head like some
great stag at bay
then lets it sink back
onto the table,
his crown too heavy
to uphold.

PART V

Threads

URBAN
(FOR RICHARD)

Street gritty, like RM Vaughan
at 3 a.m. trying to hail a cab
at the corner of Yonge and Dundas
and failing.

Your scarf sails behind you
as you peer down empty streets.
It's a flag or an emblem,
a veiled threat: *I am superior,*
it declares. *Don't challenge me.*
I could get nasty.

I won't challenge you then.
And I understand your *troubles.*
But can I tell you I can't remember
the last time I was happy?
I mean truly happy. Not just
the odd moment like when a book
was published and I was "happy"
because there weren't too
many typos.

But not "happy" as in I'm
white, male, middle-class
healthy (relatively, if you don't
count my genetic tendency
to morbidity and depression)
and intelligent.

That kind of "happy" in keeping
with the due that is supposed to

be mine when all these things are
added up. Or so I've been
    told.

In truth, I'm a misfit like you.
I don't belong anywhere.
Not even here at Yonge and
Dundas at 3 a.m.

The truth is (*Shhhh!*)
I dislike this city and much
of what it stands for but still
I have to admit, it's about as good
as it gets here in our home and
naïve land.

Torontonians aren't stupid,
we're just bland and uncultured.
It's kind of like being American,
only less colourful. So what's
the point?

And since you asked, yes,
I have tried drugs—
first the wondrous kind
as a kid then the medically
endorsed ones later.

Twice I tried anti-depressants.

They made me feel psychotic. If I was
fucked-up before, imagine what it's like
when your sense of reality
goes completely out the window.

I don't even have the luxury
of suicide, being Buddhist-minded:
"Don't throw away the Dharma.
Respect the Three Jewels."

Just what I need—more rules.

Still, I've kept true to my beliefs
all these years. I have never
made friends with an influential
person I didn't like.
I have never worked for
a multi-national corporation,
because I don't believe in greed.
If I were a hustler, I'd starve
to death before I'd fuck someone
whose ideals were compromised.

Marriage? It smacks of
real estate. You can't own
a person.

So where, you ask, has all
my integrity got me?
Nowhere. Poor. Alone.
Too late, we see the futility
of our ways. Too late, we
learn the value of utility.

Sound familiar?

At least shit brings flowers.
Or so I've been told.

Good WASP that I am,
I'll have a lot of thank-you cards
to write when all those flowers
start showing up.

So, Richard . . . RM . . . Mr. Vaughan.
Can you tell me, with your
insouciance and your clever answers
for nearly everything . . . what time
is the next streetcar
out of here?

Your scarf is brilliant, vulnerable
like a butterfly tossed about
in a snowstorm. But I've a feeling
it won't save us now.

[Richard Vaughan was a Canadian writer who committed
suicide in 2020. Among his numerous publications was the
2008 poetry collection *Troubled*, which documented his
struggles with mental illness. This poem was written in
2009, around the last time I saw Richard. –JR]

THREADS

We're all looking for those threads,
slender things, lines, memories,
that hold our lives together.

I saw a boy being beaten
outside Komrad's on Isabella Street
one summer's night. It was 1989.
Five skinheads had him
on the ground, their boots
cracking against his skull.
I was in the Living Well Café across
the street, me and a photographer
named Ralph Brodie and two
dozen others. No one else
paid any attention to what was
happening a hundred yards away.

I called the cops, but by the time
they got there the boy was gone.
He was maybe thirty. Cute, slim, blonde.
I watched him stagger up Yonge Street
all in a daze and disappear around
a corner. I told Ralph and he laughed,
called me a good citizen.

When the cops arrived, I pointed out the
skinheads. They were still there
on the curb, laughing and horsing
around. I told them where the boy had
gone. The officers shrugged it off.
They knew they were looking
at a gay bashing. Not interested.

A year later, I visited Ralph in his
studio, an old converted bowling alley.
I reminded him of the night we watched
the boy get beaten. Ralph took my
picture. We thought no more about it.

The following year, a letter appeared
in *Xtra!* A woman had written of her grief
on losing a friend, a boy who died
of a brain hemorrhage after being attacked
outside Komrad's one summer night.

That was all she knew.
She was looking for threads,
a piece of string to lead her
to the answer. If she pulled hard
enough it might unravel the secret
of where he had gone.

Times changed. I moved on, stopped
going to the clubs. I no longer
saw Ralph, though his photographs
appeared in magazines here and there.

Five years on, I was reading *Xtra!*
and saw Ralph's photograph in
Proud Lives. Dead of AIDS at 37.
I had no one to tell my story to,
no one to help unravel my secret,
the strings pulling at me again.

Twenty years passed. I found a photo
of me on a website advertising a book

about Queer Toronto photographers.
At first I couldn't recall the shot.
My hair was short, like a skinhead's.

As I pulled on the string of memory,
little by little I remembered:
that night outside Komrad's,
the boy being kicked to death,
and Ralph taking my photo.

All the threads of my life stitched together,
and me pulling and pulling on them,
the fabric of my being shredding
and coming undone.

WINDOW

This window left open,
cocked ajar just like this,
right here, right now,
bringing in the cool air,
the trickle of the fountain
in the garden below,
is the same window left ajar
in thousands of cities
on every continent
around the world,
now and before.

Why do I write poems like this?

To leave a trace,
a map for you
who follow in my steps.
To let you know I was here,
right here, thinking these thoughts
a million minutes
hours days years ago.
To say that I was
the same person
you are now
or will be tomorrow.

Outside, the leaves skew green,
push their angles up to the sky
as the day fades,
just as they have done
now and before.

Always.

Press your face against the stars
and know
I am here.

To a Would-Be LGBTQ Teen Suicide

You say you want to kill yourself
You say, *I can do this*
Because this is me
Because I am
But then you will not be *am*
Just *was*
Not even *I* anymore

You say no one
Understands me
No one knows my pain
And maybe that's true
Right now

How will you do it then?
With pills with rope or with
A bullet (if you are American)
Or maybe with fire or
Hopelessness

And who will it affect?
Your mother your father
Your sister your brother your
Neighbours your friends

Who else will it kill in turn
Like an insidious virus that
Infects everyone eventually?
Your future lovers your
Future friends me

Believe me I know
Because
I was the boy who walked

Down to the harbour at
Midnight wanting to throw
Himself in and let the sea
And sky swallow him whole
Because
I thought no one
Cared

Or maybe you are not a teenager
Maybe you are an adult
Or a senior citizen
And you think
No one could ever love you
So better to end it here
Maybe

All I know is
I was that same boy a year
Later driving along an
Unlighted road who
Thought, *Just the flick of my*
Wrist and this will all be
Over, yes I can do this
If I want to…

But no
Wait
Something saved me that day
A knowledge of the unseen
A force from above
A kind word
A poem

I don't remember now
What it was
Just an idea that

The fire in my belly
Would not burn forever
That life could taste sweet
Once more

So I clung on
My hands shaking on that
Steering wheel
My sneakers turning back
From the water lapping at
My feet at the edge

I clung on

PART VI

Two Poems for Nelson Trent Hurry

TURN

we
    exist
in this divided state
where
    what will happen
overtakes
      what comes before
we fluctuate   hesitate
stare down long hallways
waiting to turn to stone
the pound of flesh extracted
penitence
     does not come quickly

I sit and watch
       this being
       this being
divided
like a suspended sentence
      dangling
    midair
a blade   about
to drop

do you
remember the time
we rode on the Ferris wheel
watching the world
turn in our eyes

you discovered
on your arm
a spittle of vomit
from above

some child's sickness
heavy with   turning
    worlds
changing place with sky

I wiped it off your arm
you said
"most kind of you"
didn't you think
        I would die
didn't you think
    I would die
            laughing
in your arms
forever airborne
the two of us
even gravity
couldn't bring us down

I tell myself now
it is only imprecision,
    an inexactness
that keeps us apart
these things   turnings
    blades   wheels
    half-gestures
abandoning   hope
        midair
losing
                touch
I keep waiting
        the blade
    to drop

THE ONE IN THE MIRROR

it was never
my profile
lying askance   moonlight
starlit skin
gazed on
by one who loved
unquestioning
in this great universe
the joy to be
the unequivocal ecstasy
to be lying
beside you

now   in my dreams
your face takes shape
beside maps of rivers
frozen streams
my being
flows
     like glaciers
thawing
moves slow like granite
across tundra
       without sound
       without eyes
flowing
and you
      watching me sleep
a million miles away

I always wanted
I always wanted to be

    the one in the mirror

PART VII

River Run

RIVER RUN

I stood on the edge
naked
watching the river
overflow

The rain had been torrential

After you hung up that
afternoon the water spiked
the levels rising for
hours

How hard it is, you said
how hard to let go

I understand, I said
consoling and trying
to respect your choice

It's not that you wanted it,
you said, but no. Let it go.
I wasn't, clearly
I wasn't ready
to let go

So I went to the river
to wash my sins away
I went to the river
to wash my tears
away

Under the faultless moon
beneath the turbulence

I went down
I went down

I was angry
for thinking
I could save us
for thinking
you could save me

Feeling useless, like a river
with nowhere to run
thinking I have nothing
no home now
no direction

Watching
the river overflow
its banks
naked
the endless rush of water
pushing forward

With me

Its turbulence unloosed
giddy now at having
so many directions
to choose

THE RUINS OF PUERTO VALLARTA
(FOR SHANE)

March 15, 2013

Dear You

I meant to write earlier before all that absurdity about the
passport got in the way. It turns out I mislaid it after all, just as
you suggested, or perhaps a maid knocked it off my dresser.
In any case, I don't suspect treachery now, though I was
desperately worried at the time, otherwise I would never have
called at such an ungodly hour. Sorry to have woken you, but
I just couldn't think of anyone else.

Please tell Robert I'm sorry, too. He does sound lovely and is
no doubt perfect for you in ways I never was. You may be
right when you say it's not because I'm too busy, but rather
that I'm just not brave enough to meet him. Forgive me again.

It's midnight here and my first time back in five years. Also,
my first time alone. I suppose that's another thing I haven't
been able to face till now, but I thought I would try. You see,
I can be brave when I choose.

So much has changed here! It's like standing in the ruins of a
once-great city while trying to recall the splendour that was.
Earlier, I stopped by the casa we looked at all those years ago.
It seems so small now. I doubt it would have made a
successful B&B, so it's good that we didn't buy it after all.
You were right again. You would be surprised (appalled?) by
all the growth. There are condos built all the way up into the
hills, owned by rich Americans. At least that's what they say.
Who else could afford them?

The Swedes are still here. I ran into one of them on the beach, right before all the trouble. Except they're not together now. I shouldn't forget that little detail. Gay life was too tempting for them, I gather. It probably would have happened to us eventually, too, had we tried it. They still own that little art gallery off Olas Altas. It's no goldmine, I gather. They have quite a run of it in the winter, but they're hard-pressed to hold things together during the rainy months. I reminded him (Morgan, I think it was) that we met them the day they opened and bought their first painting. I'm glad you kept it, despite what I said at the time. (Have you forgiven me yet? You said you wouldn't, I know.) In any case, I hate to be reminded. I'm sure you recall how possessive I can be.

The bougainvillea are at their loveliest right now. White, pink and red blossoms everywhere. The most impressive bush is on the corner across from the hotel we stayed at, the one where we argued about ... well, about everything, really, right before it all came unraveled between us. My fault again, I know.

I stopped in that bar run by the Dutch woman and her girlfriend. You remember — it was the one where we celebrated your thirtieth birthday and had so much fun. She remembered you. Nicest man she ever met, she said. I thought that would cheer you up. Not that you need it.

The sunsets have been spectacular all week long. You recall it was what made me fall in love with this place. There were other things, of course. Like being here with you. I just didn't know it at the time. Nobody really does, do they? I suspect most of life is lived in hindsight. The best of it, anyway.

Mañana is closed. You remember that great disco with the swimming pool in the courtyard? It sounds funny to say, doesn't it? Tomorrow is closed. The future isn't what it used to be. That was a joke, I think.

I'd better finish this and go to bed. Tomorrow I'm heading to the beach to show off my new bod. I'm brave enough now to take my shirt off in public. You remember how timid I was. Not that it will do me any good. It feels like an exercise in futility. People come and go, but they never stay. I'm just proud that after all these years I've got the waistline I always wanted. Does that make me sound shallow? Oh well I can live with that. Shallow, shallow me and my plastic little heart. No great loss, I suppose.

One more week and I'll be home. It's probably all I can take, anyway. I can't say I've been a roaring success, but then I don't know what I hoped to achieve. In fact, I don't know why I bothered to come back here after all this time. I doubt I'll do it again. There comes a time in every man's life when he has to hang up the gloves and admit it's over.

I send hugs and kisses with all my love, if Robert doesn't object. Or even if he does.

Dear Me

Stalking Cool Blue

i

it is a dream   you
are there
running down corridors of blue
        cool
I see you an instant, brief
caught in shadows
    suspended   fleeing
hidden agonies
the cool corridors of
    my love

I   wait outside the door
the prophecy to come true
it's a state
in which   we all exist
            sometime

ii

it is about the sea
    this dream   I have
standing on the shore
outward   looking
fistfuls of shell
        falling
through wet fingers, strains
the interiors
    echoing
with   stamp of   eternal

later, in places where I reside
the interiors   bright
like cut glass
     reflect   resound
with the sound of   empty

this is what it is like
to have   killed
an angry word no different
than a violent deed
     a child
pulling the wings off
     a butterfly
a bullet could not destroy more

iii

it is about escaping, holding
of head in one's hands
the shuffling
          of expressions: this
for the paperboy, this
the grocer, the bank teller
another for the friend with
discerning eye

hiding in the pale blue flame
of being
     just beyond
     battlefields of the mind
and hearts stuck up on gateposts
a bit too obvious
for the neighbours' stare
the dripping, bleeding
on sidewalk and lawn

(I pretend I am taking out the trash
in the morning and back in on my way
home from work)

iv

in the night
when the little ones are asleep
propriety breaks over the lawn
    great waves crashing
over pebbles
        thrashing of pillows
shifting, moving, re-arranging
to discover the endless possibilities
    of what is gone
and how many ways
can you spell e-m-p-t-y
without giving it a note
too resounding

louder than the inside
of shells, the quiet rooms
we enter alone
and shut the door
on
    the unfinished past
creeping
always behind us,
just

v

it is about waking: to find
        yourself
conversing drearily
over the same old argument

that has already been decided
like the wave and crest of sea
the peculiar rhythm of placement
and displacement
the ineluctable absence
                that comes
treading down the long night
exorcising the ghosts of old loves
as nothing more
than an accident on the pillow

it is about rising: to the
        sound of bells
and feet running down
empty streets
        only to embrace
                nothing

WINTER GARDEN

these lovers on the grass
the older boy lying, relaxed
    his younger, lithe companion
    whispering next to him
about the greenness of life
the granaries full of grain
don't they see the vines
curling above, arteries
emptying abruptly, the
    dreadful arching of leaves
    all around, can't
    they hear the wind shrieking
    the clouds to a bitter autumn,
and know how soon at the window
    they too will howl
when winter comes

ODE TO A DEAD LOVER
(FOR MICHAEL RIDLER)

In a dream you came to me.
It's been so long, I said.
Yes, you answered — a long time dead.
Then you laughed
as only you could laugh.

We spoke of this and that.
I made a bad joke
and you tipped your glass in jest.
Its contents spilled cool
against my skin. Stop it,
I said. You know I hate getting wet.

You nodded and smiled
standing over me, legs askew
like a captain on a doomed ship.

What about love? you asked.
And all that passed between us.
Do you remember?
Of course, I replied. (It was a love letter
that had brought you to me then, but
you'd changed the words.
Always editing me, I thought.
Here we go again.)

I'm interested in that boy, I said,
at least now that you're gone.
He's not for you, you replied.
Too young? I asked.
No, too old. You forget! What's up
is down, what's down is up. That's just
how it goes on this side of things.

I closed my eyes, afraid
to reach out, afraid to feel
the emptiness between us
and know the divide
was greater than I thought.

Are you still angry with me? I asked.
Yes, you said, turning to leave.
And you? Still afraid to touch?

ICE FIELDS
(FOR UMAIR)

I think of Robert Scott
on his icebound expedition
to the pole, and stop to wonder:
when did fear clutch
his throat and say
You will not return?

So I gather my strength
for this journey
as you tie up your snowshoes
against the buoyant ecstasy
to be had

This coy escape you contemplate
with me, twenty years your senior
when we touch
this challenge you give me to love
you while hinting at the marvels
to be had

I gaze longingly at your thighs
the dark chestnuts of
your nipples, sweet apples
of your sex, a staff
planted in ice

I ride you like a whale harpooned
a ghost ship caught in ice
erasing boundaries
one floe at a time

I watch you plant your flag
for country and glory—that
man-thing we do
claiming lost continents
before moving on to new territory
unknown ground, fresh kill

PART VIII

Someday We'll Be Together

CONUNDRUM WITH WAVES
(PROVINCETOWN 11-09-16)

It is the eternal
     moment
this moment that is now
   that is forever
gone
   already

As
the sea of life fills
       the
space
   between your toes
in the sand
 between your feet
   the water
sluicing and shushing
its way in and out

No ending or beginning
  giving and taking
bringing you with it now
to your desired   end
which is also your beginning
which is not
    now

But which is
  all we have
really and here we
go
   again

So all is all

In this moment
    in these waves
    in this nothingness

That never
    ceases

NICHOLAS

It didn't take long, did it?
On the other hand, it must have
taken you years to fully arrive.
They won't understand
how you needed to follow your mother.
She went away too soon, leaving you
and your sister Frieda alone to grieve
over her dead body—head
in the stove, the rest of her
on the kitchen floor. As if she wanted
to set her head on fire.
What an image to leave you with!

She went away too soon.
You must have thought she took
too long coming home
so you had to go and find her,
to bring her back with a resounding
crash, just one more victim
of her fame. Posthumous, of course.

I think how you must have
flayed yourself with her lost love,
all those feelings taking you down
to her, Euridyce in her Underworld,
to that place where myth and dreams
collide. Her mother-myth
taking you down: Goodbye!
Goodbye dear. I won't be long.
But, oh, it's messy down here!

Just her and her father, dark Sisyphus,
the two of them forever rolling their stones
uphill and down. Now here's your father,

Terrible Ted, and all of the dead
rising up like balloons to greet you:
home at last!

It's your time now. Hold on, you're
nearly there. You'll see her
soon. Go on. Speak to her.
Tell her what she did:
Goddess, mother, monster—all
she left you was a handful of poems,
balloons not even real.

DISSOLVE

I tell my editor
I want a jump cut here or
maybe a quick
dissolve to show
time passing
things changing, transforming
these lives, these
people on the screen

They don't matter
they're only lives on a screen
but you and me, we're different
we can't end up where we started
every time

We
move forward,
one way only
not like these flickering lights

Our solid bodies moving
through empty space
as
we dissolve

THE LOVE OF THE HUNTER FOR THE STAG

My heart leaps out of my mouth
like a deer startled in a field
leaping and bounding in surprise
before turning back to stare
at the ineluctable hunter
who has come to take him home.

In you, I look for the wounding
again and again, but cannot find it.
I bleed, yet my wounds are clean.
Hunter, ride your stag. Take me down.

METABOLIC

Sitting here on my turquoise
mid-century sofa, more a
love-seat, really, permanently
separated from its other half,
reading Elizabeth Bishop (*The
Complete Poems*) in a failed
attempt to drown out the noise
of the construction next door
and with music playing (upping
the ante, the frantic seesaw
of sound) when suddenly—
the worker's buzz-saw cuts
right through my wall in
perfect harmony with the
Josquin mass I am playing.
What does it mean then that
the buzz-saw is in perfect
harmony with the strands of
Josquin and the words of
Elizabeth Bishop, the
destruction and construction
coming together as one?

TEACHING MY SON TO BE

At night, I say
repeat after me:

You are I, I tell him
raising one finger in the air
and the other pointing at his
small chest

I am
I think
I feel
I do

He wiggles and squirms,
makes faces at the
strange sounds, laughs
at the giant clown man
who looks down at him
in his crib, a ship
setting sail on a wide
sea for places unknown
and lands unexplored

I watch

Waiting for day, he climbs
down into sleep, the
place where all things
happen

The place where
It's easy to be

I am
I think
I feel
I do

All around, soft shapes
collide in the air—a star,
a seahorse, a cow—
here in this place
where nothing else matters

In the morning, when he wakes
we repeat the game:

You are I, I tell him

I am
I think
I feel
I do

I love

Someday We'll Be Together
(For Aunt Evie)

Auntie, where did you live
when you lived in the Donovan?

I remember a second-storey walk-up,
a cold-water flat on a dingy side street
where I first learned to smoke cigarettes
and eat BLTs on rye bread

I looked for it again when I was in town
going round and round for ages
only I couldn't find it
it was like it had never been there

I wanted to say, this is where my
cousin Diane and I hung out as kids,
trying to be cool, showing off my rough past
to a new boyfriend
we were poor then, we were so ghetto
how she told me her father had left
but would come back from time to time
hanging around
drunk on the stairs

Cousin Diane who taught me to smoke
and who would die in two-months' time
from lung cancer at fifty

This was my childhood, I wanted to say
a reflection of Beatles-era England,
Motown, and late rock'n'roll USA
those summers of bangling pop tunes
on a transistor radio held chest high
where did they go?

And my older cousin, a boy-hunter
who looked at me and declared "you're cute"
and me blushing because I didn't know it
"Suzanne's gone boy crazy" they used to say
"It's why she failed grade eight"
she couldn't keep her mind on things
though what things, they never said

And her father, Edgar, a cab driver
a gentle man we called Uncle Cigar
for his bad habits, also dead before his time
going without a complaint
"Didn't want to worry us," Sue said
"Thought he was being a bother—if only, eh?
Might still be alive today"

"C'mon—let's go see the Big Nickel,"
she would say, and me asking her
which boyfriend would drive us there?

It was sort of a joke, but I liked it all the same,
like being allowed to hold the radio
with all those songs: Herman's Hermits,
Dave Clark Five

And Smokey Robinson shining through
around every other corner, Diana Ross
and her Supremes catching up to him

Like me and Suzanne and Diane forever

ACKNOWLEDGMENTS

My thanks to the Ontario Arts Council for a grant that helped with writing some of the earlier pieces included here, as well as to those who gave suggestions in shaping a number of these works so long ago that they may not remember, though I do: Dawn Rae Downton and Linda Spalding. I would also like to offer my gratitude to my editor, Louis Flint Ceci, whose hands have carefully tended and guided this collection along the way.

ABOUT THE AUTHOR

Jeffrey Round was born in Sudbury, Ontario, and grew up in Windsor and Halifax. He is an award-winning author, film-maker, and song writer. His breakout novel, *A Cage of Bones*, based in part on his experiences as a model in Europe's fashion industry, was listed on AfterElton's 50 Best Gay books. *Lake on the Mountain*, the first in a seven-book series featuring missing-persons investigator Dan Sharp, won a Lambda Award for Best Gay Mystery. His short film, *My Heart Belongs to Daddy*, won awards for Best Canadian Director and Best Use of Music, among others. *In the Museum of Leonardo da Vinci*, his previous poetry collection, was nominated for a ReLit Award. In 2021 he took top juried prizes around the world for his music video, *Don't You Think I Know*. He lives in Toronto. For more information and to hear his music go to www.jeffreyround.com.

CPSIA information can be obtained
at www.ICGtesting.com
Printed in the USA
BVHW042356141022
649426BV00001B/78

9 781734 738995